JERRY BRONDFIELD

D0036642

SCHOLASTIC BOOK SERVICES
New York Toronto London Auckland Sydney Tokyo

ISBN 0-590-31623-0

12 11 10 9 8 7 6 5 4 3 2 1   9   0 1 2 3 4 5/8

Printed in the U. S. A.   06

CONTENTS

ALL-PRO OFFENSE 1979

WR: **John Jefferson**, San Diego Chargers
WR: **John Stallworth**, Pittsburgh Steelers
 TE: **Dave Casper**, Oakland Raiders
  T: **Leon Gray**, Houston Oilers
  T: **Marvin Powell**, New York Jets
  G: **John Hannah**, New England Patriots
  G: **Joe DeLamielleure**, Buffalo Bills
  C: **Mike Webster**, Pittsburgh Steelers
  Q: **Dan Fouts**, San Diego Chargers
 RB: **Earl Campbell**, Houston Oilers
 RB: **Ottis Anderson**, St. Louis Cardinals

Wide Receiver
JOHN JEFFERSON
6-1, 184
SAN DIEGO CHARGERS

Right now, one of the finest if not THE finest passing combinations in the NFL is Dan Fouts to John Jefferson. Fouts, the Chargers QB, knows that any time he needs a big hunk of yardage fast, all he has to say to Jefferson in the huddle is: "Okay Jeff, get loose, hang loose, give 'em a head shake and I'll present you with the ball."

Charger fans — and a lot of people throughout the league — knew it was going to happen from Jefferson's rookie year on. He was a unanimous All-Rookie choice in 1978 and all-pro stardom was a cinch for the future.

His stats for last season are dazzling: 1,090 yards and 61 completions, and 10 touchdowns. That spells "danger" to any secondary defense, no matter how you look at it.

As a rookie he'd been the first NFL newcomer to gain at least 1,000 yards receiving in almost 10 years (since the Eagles' Harold Jackson in 1969). The Chargers drafted him after he'd caught 175 passes for 2,824 yards at Arizona State....They checked the films, saw his blazing speed and the nifty way he ran pass routes, and all the coaches whistled at once....There was no doubt in anyone's mind that Jefferson would make the starting team from game one....He did, of course, and his game plan is to scare defensive backs out of their wits — and their shoes, too!

JOHN STALLWORTH

6-2, 183

PITTSBURGH STEELERS

Yes, we know that Lynn Swann also is a wide receiver for the Steelers. Yes, we know that Lynn Swann has been an All-Pro for many years. Yes, we know some of you will be surprised that this year Swann has been beaten out by his teammate for All-Pro honors.

That's because nobody can overlook the super season Stallworth has had. But the figures alone don't tell the story: 1,183 yards, 66 completions, a gaudy 18.7 yards per catch, and eight TDs. If you watched Stallworth on TV in the playoffs and in the Super Bowl, you know what speed he has, and great hands, and the ability to beat the defender on the bomb. Stallworth has been doing that for years, and finally people have caught on to the fact that there simply isn't anyone better than he is. Incidentally, he has caught touchdown passes in six straight playoff games.

Stallworth was only a fourth-round draft choice by the Steelers in 1974, out of Alabama A&M, but he made greater progress than any rookie receiver that first year. A series of injuries slowed him down for a couple of seasons, but by 1977 he had regained his true stardom. As Terry Bradshaw's favorite receiver, he is the most dangerous threat in the NFL on the long, game-breaking play.

Tight End
DAVE CASPER
6-4, 230
OAKLAND RAIDERS

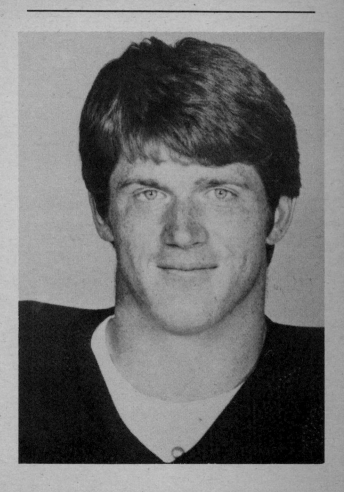

Probably no pro team ever had two such tight ends playing at the same time as do the Raiders. It was tough to choose between Dave Casper and Raymond Chester, but Casper, who'd been All-Pro three straight years, is the choice again because of consistency. A champ is the champ until absolutely proven otherwise, right?

The trouble with Dave Casper is that he doesn't look spectacular, even while he's doing an amazing job.

"There's just no one better at all phases of his job," say the Raider coaches of the former Notre Dame All-America. "If he's just called upon to block, he explodes out of there and knocks his man right out of the play. If the assignment calls for him to block his man first, and then run his pass route, he does it, bang-bang. He hits, releases off his man, and next thing you know he's slipping into the seams of the zone coverage. He gets open as slick as any tight end I've seen."

There's one other thing. Or two. Casper has great hands for the ball. And once he tucks it away he's like a bull elephant. The secondary has to converge on him mighty fast, because it usually takes two to bring him down.

He doesn't have great speed, but he doesn't waste his moves. He knows where he's going at all times and when he and the ball arrive there together, the Raiders drive is another 10 or 15 yards closer to the goal line. His 57 catches for 771 yards and three touchdowns are true All-Pro stats.

Offensive Tackle
LEON GRAY
6-3, 260
HOUSTON OILERS

Leon Gray is one of those rare players who has made All-Pro with two different teams. His first all-star selection was in 1978 with New England. Traded to the Oilers last season he picked up right where he'd left off. No one was more pleased than the Oiler coaching staff who watched him block ferociously and put out such great pass protection for Oiler QB Dan Pastorini.*

But football almost lost Gray to music. When Leon Gray played the trumpet in his Mississippi high school band, he was excused from 10 band appearances each year. Those were the Friday nights he played tackle for the football team. Gray took his football skills to Jackson State College, Mississippi, but left his trumpet home.

Gray started for four years at Jackson and became a third-round draft choice by the Miami Dolphins. The Dolphins soon made a mistake. They cut him in camp and put him out for waivers. The New England Patriots grabbed him right after the final cut.

Gray started the last eight games of the year for the Patriots as a rookie. He was definitely one of the NFL's future stars.

Soon Gray became known for his pass-blocking abilities. He was already a powerful blocker on running plays. Throughout the NFL, the defenses knew it wasn't going to be easy getting through to sack his team's QB.

"He was my life insurance," said Pastorini. "He helped give me the confidence to stay an extra split-second in the pocket. Often it's the difference between a completion, an incompletion, or an interception." Or in getting the QB's head knocked off.

*Traded to Raiders.

Offensive Tackle
MARVIN POWELL
6-5, 271
NEW YORK JETS

Marvin Powell enjoys reading poetry and listening to classical music, but nobody in football pads ever mistakes him for a sweet and gentle soul. Uh-uh. Not Marvin. Not the way he explodes into a blocking assignment or hauls that huge body of his into pass protection for his QB.

The All-America from Southern California was a first-round draft choice for the Jets in 1977 and he immediately won a starting assignment. Along with Chris Ward of Ohio State at the other tackle they were known as "the book-ends." Both won prominent all-rookie recognition, and two years later Powell was definitely an All-Pro.

Powell, who played in three Rose Bowl for the Trojans, started out as a tight end but was switched to tackle in his second collegiate season. With the Jets he was tabbed as a tackle all the way. Not only is he a master technician in his blocking assignments but he keeps in such super condition that he never seems to tire.

Powell, whose nickname is "Boomer," comes from aggressive stock. His father sneaked into the army at age 15 in World War II and fought in the invasion of Normandy, became a career officer and also fought in the Korean War.

JOHN HANNAH

6-2, 265

NEW ENGLAND PATRIOTS

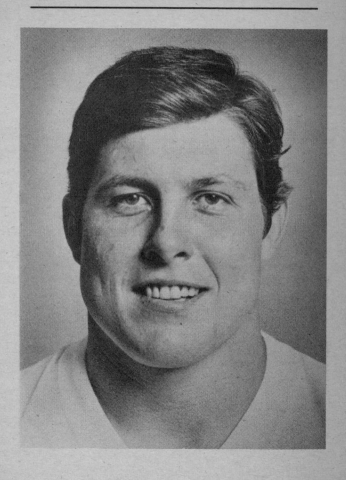

A lot of fans think this will be comeback year for the Patriots. But one Patriot has never been away. This is the fourth straight time John Hannah has been named All-Pro and it's a habit he doesn't want broken.

A lot of the Patriot's ground-gaining came over Hannah's position, where he was a tremendous straight-ahead blocker. But Hannah carried out his other chores equally well. He was super at pulling out to block on wide plays, and he gave QB Steve Grogan excellent protection on passes.

Some people thought Hannah would have trouble in the pros after starring at Alabama. Because Alabama used a wishbone offense, Hannah did all his blocking straight ahead. What would happen when he had to do so many different things in the pros? But 'Bama coach Bear Bryant said Hannah was the best lineman he'd ever had. "Don't worry about ol' Ham Hocks (Hannah's nick-name)," said Bryant, "He'll do it all."

Bryant was right, of course. Hannah became a starter as a rookie and made the All-Rookie team after being drafted on the first round in 1973. Except for one game in his first season, he's started every game for the Patriots since then. Look for more All-Pro years for ol' Ham Hocks.

JOE DeLAMIELLEURE
6-3, 250
BUFFALO BILLS

When some rookies come to the NFL, experts say: "He can't miss." But they do. When Joe DeLamielleure came up they said: "Not only is he going to make it, but he'll be All-Pro some day." This guy didn't disappoint anybody. This is his fifth straight year as the best in the business.

When the Bills' DeLamielleure was at Michigan State he majored in criminal justice. "I wish he'd have gone into crime busting instead of football," said an NFL linebacker. "When he comes out to lead interference you can just see that steely glint in his eye as he concentrates on getting his man. And he nearly always does."

A first-round draft choice in 1973, De-Lamielleure became an immediate starter for the Bills and made the All-Rookie team. It took him only two years to make the jump to All-Pro. But the way he leads interference and drops back for pass protection, everyone agreed he'd make it soon. He's also a ferocious straight-ahead blocker on running plays. "I loved to run behind Joe," said O.J. Simpson, who once played for the Bills. "He's the kind of blocker a ballcarrier should remember in his will."

DeLamielleure three times made the All-Big Ten team in college, and topped it off with All-America in his senior year.

Joe has one more distinction going for him. He has one of the toughest names to spell in the entire NFL. If you don't believe it, take another look.

Center
MIKE WEBSTER
6-1½, 250
PITTSBURGH STEELERS

It's the second straight year for Webster and he may make it a habit. If you want one word for Webster it's "steady." Make it two words: ROCK STEADY.

The Steelers didn't select Mike Webster until the sixth round of the draft a few years ago—which isn't very high. But the Steelers' coaches had him figured for two positions: guard or center. That way he had two chances. Actually he made good at both. He was an All-Rookie choice at center, but a year later, in 1976, he split the season at both posts. The following season he became the Steelers' center — for good. And better than good is the way to describe the former Wisconsin star.

He handles all snaps, not just to the quarterback but the longer ones for punts and place-kicks. Many centers can't do that. And when getting it into QB Terry Bradshaw's hands, he's a master of split-second timing. It's the best exchange in the NFL.

After the snap, Webster blocks with great ferocity and quickness. Even when the defense plays a man right over him, he isn't afraid of the slap to the head which centers must expect. He also has two other talents. He has the quick feet needed when a center drops back to give his QB pass protection. And on punts, after snapping the ball, he's one of the first downfield to close in on the punt returner. What it adds up to is All-Pro performance without weakness.

Quarterback
DAN FOUTS
6-3, 205
SAN DIEGO CHARGERS

Okay, Ken Stabler, Bob Griese, Terry Bradshaw and a couple other of you guys. Move over. There's been a new kid on the block, pushing you for attention, and he's finally arrived.

You don't see any of the Chargers wearing Super Bowl rings, but they all know—and so do a lot of fans—that their own Dan Fouts was the best all-around QB in the business. And why not? After all, little Danny Fouts, as a 12-year-old started early in pro football as a ball boy for the San Francisco 49ers. Naturally, he dreamed that some day he'd be promoted to QB for somebody.

At the University of Oregon he passed for 5,995 yards and 37 touchdowns, and was an All-Pacific Coast QB. The Chargers made him a first-round draft choice in 1973. He had perfect dimensions for a QB —6-3, 205 pounds, and had quick, nimble feet in setting up. Then there was the rifle arm, the soft touch when needed, and a quick release. All he needed was experience, and the Chargers saw to it that he started several times in his rookie season. A year later he was the regular. But even with a so-so team he was hailed as a budding star. Then, for three straight seasons he was one of the few NFL QBs who went over 50% in completions.

Last season, with an improving supporting cast, Fouts took the Chargers into the playoffs for the first time. Although the Chargers, as a team, had finally jelled, nearly all the NFL coaches and critics said it was the all-around brilliance of Fouts which carried them so far. A narrow 17-14 loss to the powerful Houston Oilers, in a first-round divisional playoff, halted the Chargers' bid for a Super Bowl slot.

For the year, Fouts had dazzling stats of 530 passing attempts, 332 completions, a 62.6 percentage, 4,082 total yards and 26 TDs. He led the NFL in attempts, completions, completion percentage, total yards, and was fifth in TD tosses with 24.

19

EARL CAMPBELL

5-11, 224

HOUSTON OILERS

It was the same Earl Campbell, only more of the same! The All-Everything, All-World rookie of 1978 continued in 1979

where he had left off. No, sir! That rookie season had been no fluke! Yes, sir! He proved himself the second time around!

Listen to Dwight White of the Steelers: "Earl Campbell is almost illegal. When he hits that hole it's like a door slamming. Earl Campbell is a Larry Csonka and O.J. Simpson combined." Some of the things other players say about the Oilers' rookie aren't printable.

Any way you look at it, Earl Campbell is the most exciting runner in the NFL in years. A unanimous All-America at the University of Texas, the Heisman winner was the Oilers' first draft pick two years ago after rushing for 4,444 yards as a Longhorn. Oh, he was super, all right, but would he bring all that talent to the pros? He brought it—and it was the reason the Oilers made the playoffs for the first time in their history in 1978.

Moving like a runaway freight train, Campbell uses his brute power and great speed to run around tacklers or run over them if he has to. Often he is hit by three or four people, but breaks the tackles and continues on for four, five, or ten yards more. Defensive backs find his speed deceptive. He would be into the secondary before they are set to hit him. And often it is too late.

Campbell's league-leading 1,697 yards and 19 TDs for 1979, coming after his super-rookie season, put him squarely on a course to break the legendary Jim Brown's lifetime mark of 12,312 yards.

Running Back
OTTIS ANDERSON
6-1, 210
ST. LOUIS CARDINALS

Whatever happened to Walter Payton, you ask? Nothing at all. The Chicago Bears' Payton is still one of the greatest running backs ever to pull on a pair of cleats.... But last year there was NOBODY better than the Cards' sensational rookie. (Well, maybe Earl Campbell, right?)

The big, fast, hard-running rookie from Miami of Florida, was about the only thing St. Louis fans could cheer about last fall, and they were lucky the Cardinals got him as a first-round draft choice. At Miami, in his senior season, he rushed for 1,266 yards on 224 carries for a dazzling 5.6 per carry, and had a string of four straight 100-yard games. From the moment Anderson appeared in the Cardinals' pre-season camp he was a marked man.

"He'll be a starter," said one sports writer. "You're not being kind enough to him," said another writer. "He's going to be a superstar." Well, he certainly was all of that in his first season, and was one of the rare rookie running backs ever to make All-Pro. A fast, bruising runner, it's a dangerous job bringing him down, one-on-one. St. Louis fans say that if he had the Pittsburgh Steelers, or Dallas Cowboys offensive line in front of him he'd run for more than 2,000 yards per season. Instead of his merely sensational 1,605 yards and eight touchdowns as a rookie. A nice thought, even if it can't happen.

ALL-PRO DEFENSE 1979

- E: **Lee Roy Selmon**, Tampa Bay Buccaneers
- E: **Jack Youngblood**, Los Angeles Rams
- T: **Randy White**, Dallas Cowboys
- T: **Larry Brooks**, Los Angeles Rams
- LB: **Randy Gradishar**, Denver Broncos
- LB: **Robert Brazile**, Houston Oilers
- LB: **Jack Ham**, Pittsburgh Steelers
- CB: **Lemar Parrish**, Washington Redskins
- CB: **Louis Wright**, Denver Broncos
- S: **Mike Reinfeldt**, Houston Oilers
- S: **Donnie Shell**, Pittsburgh Steelers

Defensive End
LEE ROY SELMON
6-3, 255
TAMPA BAY BUCCANEERS

It's a big jump from college stardom to success as a pro, and it's a risky business pinning "can't miss" labels on a rookie. There was no risk when they pinned it on Lee Roy Seldom. One of three All-America brothers at Oklahoma, Selmon was a first-round draft choice for the new team Bucs four years ago. His strength and agility made him an instant starter and won him All-Rookie acclaim.

Two years later he was being seriously considered for All-Pro status. Last year there was no way anyone could keep him off the honor team. "He's the best defensive end against the run I've ever seen," says Buc coach John McKay. True, true! Nobody puts a full block on him when he's angling in on the ball carrier. And once he gets his hands on the guy, the guy has gone as far as he's going on that play.

Selmon is a fierce pass rusher. As often as not he goes right over the blocker on his way to the quarterback, instead of circling around him. Once, against the Buffalo Bills, he actually threw two blockers into the Bills' QB, Joe Ferguson, to make the sack. "Most amazing defensive play I ever saw," said Buffalo sports writer, Larry Felser.

Give Lee Roy Selmon a little more time, Larry, and he'll make some even more amazing plays. After all, he hasn't even reached his prime.

Defensive End

JACK YOUNGBLOOD
6-4, 242
LOS ANGELES RAMS*

The fact that the Rams this year will be moving from Los Angeles to neighboring Anaheim simply means that Jack Youngblood will be picking up additional fans in the Disneyland area. For years Angelinos have been screaming that Youngblood had been getting gypped. He'd been named to several Pro Bowl squads but his local cheer-leaders insisted he should also be All-Pro.

Youngblood finally made All-Pro in 1978, and the way he played last season there was nobody around who was going to stop him from repeating.

A first-round draft choice from the University of Florida in 1971, Youngblood was a starter almost from the beginning. He's known to be particularly rough on QBs dropping back to pass. He rarely gets fully blocked out of the play, and he terrorizes the ball carriers. Nobody can recall the last time he failed to contain a sweep. The guy kicking extra points against the Rams usually has one eye on the monster making a rush at him from the corner. What we're talking about is the complete defensive end, right?

During the off-season, Youngblood works for a bank credit-card company. But nobody gets more credit than Jack Youngblood among the NFL's defensive ends.

*Moving to Anaheim for 1980.

Defensive Tackle
RANDY WHITE
6-4, 252
DALLAS COWBOYS

When Randy White made All-Pro for the first time in 1978 he decided he liked the honor so much that he'd go for two straight. And the way he performed last year you get the idea that he wants to make a habit of it. Don't bet against three straight.

White has been around, defensively, but now he has finally found a home. He was an All-America defensive end at Maryland, but when the Cowboys made him a first-round draft choice five years ago, they made him a linebacker. Why not? He was big, strong, and very agile. In fact he was downright quick. And mean. And determined. And intense. And he liked to hit ball carriers. See what we mean?

But although he started some games his first two years, he also served as a back-up. Coach Tom Landry decided on a switch. Because of his quickness and great strength, White would also make a great pass rusher at tackle, where he could be used all the time.

So, Randy White, in 1977, went into his third defensive position. He took to the job immediately and had a great season.

But 1978 saw him developing into a superstar. Quarterbacks around the league were fleeing for their lives as White put the pressure on them. When he wasn't sacking them he was making them get rid of the ball before they really wanted to. Meanwhile, he was making his share of tackles. Blockers rarely made him take a backward step.

What Randy White had become was the perfect defensive tackle and a big reason for the Cowboys' march to greatness.

LARRY BROOKS
6-3, 255
LOS ANGELES RAMS

    Larry Brooks, who made All-Pro for the first time in 1977, missed out the following season. But he was determined that he wouldn't be known as a one-year fluke, so last season he was a terror again on the field.

Off the field Larry Brooks is the quiet, conservative type. He even works in a bank during the off-season. You can't be much quieter and conservative than that. He's also a perfect example of the athlete who goes further than most people expect. Mostly because of great determination.

Brooks was the Rams 14th-round draft choice from little-known Virginia State. Even without a lot of press clippings he'd shown enough for the Rams to take a chance on him. For an athlete like Larry Brooks, that's all he wanted. In training camp in 1972, he did things rookies usually don't do. Like smashing running plays aimed at him in the very first scrimmage. Half way through his rookie year he was a starter. Then, bad luck struck. Half way through the 1975 season he had knee surgery. End of the road?

Not for Larry Brooks. He built the knee back up and in 1976 he was chosen for his first Pro Bowl berth. In 1977 he was truly a star.

"He rarely makes a wrong move," says an admiring pro coach. "In other words, you can't beat him by waiting for him to make a mistake. You've got to just old-fashioned overpower him."

Larry Brooks doesn't overpower easily. He has great strength, especially in his upper arms, which enables him to shuck off the blockers. They say he doesn't look spectacular. You don't have to when you get the job done, anyway.

Linebacker
RANDY GRADISHAR
6-3, 233
DENVER BRONCOS

You might call Randy Gradishar, Mr. Perpetual Motion. If you've seen him play on TV you've seen him flying all over the place — in on virtually every play.

Randy Gradishar plays the middle linebacker spot for the Broncos, which means he has to cover a lot of ground. Anything that comes over the middle or to either side of him is his responsibility. If the outside linebackers get fooled or taken out of the play, the middle man has to cover. With his great speed and zest for the ball, Gradishar seems to be in all places at once.

He attracted all the pro scouts' attention as an All-America at Ohio State. Woody Hayes, the Buckeyes' famed former coach, tagged him as "...the best linebacker I've ever seen." He'd been a three-year starter for the Bucks and an All-America, but the Bronco coaches held their breath a bit. He'd had a complicated knee operation after his final college season and only time would tell if it were successful. Other clubs decided to pass him up. The Broncos gambled and grabbed him on the first round of the 1974 draft.

The knee held up. Gradishar got in a lot of playing time his rookie year and became a starter—and a star—in his second season. He has been the Broncos' leader in tackles the last three seasons. And with his speed and savvy he's a dangerous defender against the pass.

This is Gradishar's second time as an All-Pro. It won't be his last.

Linebacker
ROBERT BRAZILE
6-4, 230
HOUSTON OILERS

Bob Brazile made All-Pro in his second season, in 1976, and has been steamed ever since. That's because the selectors left him off the honor team the next two years and he's been battling to prove them wrong. Brazile's battle is over. He's back where most folks think he belongs.

When the Oilers made Brazile, of Jackson State in Mississippi, their first draft choice in 1975, some experts said, "he'll make the pro's All-Rookie team, for sure." Others said, "He'll not only make All-Rookie, but in his second season he'll be All-Pro." Everybody was right.

Tremendously quick for his size, he also has great strength in his hands and arms, and has the ability to shuck off blockers who are trying to get him out of the play.

"But if it weren't for his strength and speed," says an opposing coach, "he could do it just as well with his smarts. I never saw a linebacker come into the league and learn his trade so quickly. He still plays like a five-year veteran, yet he still has the enthusiasm of a youngster. It's obvious he loves what he's doing."

What he does so well is sack the quarterback, stack up the run, and defend slickly against the short pass. There just isn't any more that can be asked of a linebacker. If they ever invent a new demand, Bob Brazile will fill it.

Linebacker
JACK HAM
6-1, 225
PITTSBURGH STEELERS

Jack Ham on the All-Pro team ... ? So what else is new? It's a yearly thing, like the return of the robins. Maybe, when he's old and gray, somebody will beat him out, but don't count on it.

"Jack Ham, on any play," says a veteran NFL scout, "is always where he's supposed to be, and when he's supposed to be. You can count on it as surely as the sun rises in the east."

And he could have added: "He's also doing what he's supposed to do to the ball carrier or pass receiver, which is laying a furious pair of hands on him."

If you took a poll of all NFL coaches, Jack Ham would no doubt be voted the greatest linebacker in football today. Because of Ham and a few others who come close to him in ability, linebackers have become some of the most glamorous players in the NFL.

Wayne Walker, who once starred for the Detroit Lions, says: "Linebackers are usually among the most intelligent players on your team. They have to be able to make the many adjustments the position calls for. They have to defend against the run and the pass and be able to smell out which it's going to be when so many plays start out the same way. Then they've got to have the speed and mental agility to adjust. And all the while they're taking a beating from blockers while their attention is elsewhere."

That's Jack Ham. Ham was an All-America at Penn State in 1970. The Steelers made him their second-round draft pick in 1971 and he rewarded them by making the starting lineup as a rookie. He's not big as linebackers go — only 6-1 and 225 pounds—but he makes up for it in intelligence, quickness, and alertness.

Cornerback
LEMAR PARRISH
5-10, 183
WASHINGTON REDSKINS

Lemar Parrish is testimony to the value of good, old-fashioned American "plugging away." Parrish believed in himself and kept working at being the best cornerback in the NFL. It took him 10 years to convince the experts he was All-Pro material and last year he made it after being selected for the Pro Bowl six times.

Parrish broke into the NFL as merely a seventh-round draft choice with the Cincinnati Bengals in 1970 and by the following season he was a regular, and a rising star. Bengal fans were shocked when he was traded to Washington in 1978 but Redskin fans were delighted from his very first game with the 'Skins.' A teeth-rattling tackler with a nose for the ball, he protected his zone against enemy passes with all-out fury.

He also broke his hand in the eighth game of that first season with Washington but after three weeks of rest he insisted that he be put back in the line-up wearing a cast on his hand. He played the last three games of the season that way.

A product of little Lincoln College, in Missouri, Parrish last season was so dazzling that there was no way anyone could leave him off the honor team.

Cornerback
LOUIS WRIGHT
6-2, 195
DENVER BRONCOS

What does it take to be an All-Pro cornerback? Well, it isn't enough to just have toughness, great speed, and hitting ability. You also have to have great reflexes and instincts. Rich McCabe, coach of the Broncos' defensive backs, says Louie Wright has some of the fastest reflexes in the NFL. "I've never seen a defensive back who can recover so quickly when what looks like a run turns into a pass, or vice versa. For Louie there isn't a split second of lost motion when he has to make the switch.

"His great reflexes and instincts show up, too, when a pass receiver tries to burn him with a quick cut on a pass route. He thinks he's shaken Louie, but Louie doesn't get lost very easily. I always have confidence that Louie will recover to bat down the ball or intercept it."

Wright, a star collegian at Long Beach State, California, is also the Broncos' fastest player with a sizzling 4.4. for 40 yards. In college he ran the 100 in 9.6 and was an All-Coast selection. The Broncos didn't wait very long to grab him in the draft. He was only the second player in Denver history to be snatched up as a first-round choice. And now that he's made All-Pro for the second straight year, mark him down as a fixture that way for the future.

MIKE REINFELDT
6-2, 195
HOUSTON OILERS

For years, Cliff Harris and Charlie Waters of the Dallas Cowboys have had a strangle-hold on the safety positions on the All-Pro secondaries. Now it's time for new faces — and one of the brightest to appear is the Oilers' Mike Reinfeldt. You wouldn't have given much for his chances back in his rookie days in 1976.

First of all, he came out of the University of Wisconsin-Milwaukee (NOT the biggie Wisconsin Badgers of Madison). And Wisc-Mil was never noted for football players. In fact, Reinfeldt couldn't get drafted in an open doorway. He had to walk in and tell the Oilers he deserved a look as a free agent.

The Oilers looked and their coaches exchanged meaningful glances when they saw Reinfeldt knocking heads. "Natural instincts," glowed Bum Phillips, the Oiler coach. And in his first season, Reinfeldt made second team All-Rookie.

The following season as a "one-year veteran" he was close to stardom according to every expert in the NFL. Last year he began intimidating pass receivers and ball carriers wherever there was an unfriendly jersey in his neighborhood. Ferocious as he is on the field he's a bit more gentlemanly in his hobbies off the field: tennis and golf. But they tell us he still knocks the cover off the ball.

Safety
DONNIE SHELL
5-11, 190
PITTSBURGH STEELERS

On defense, everyone talks about the Steelers' Iron Curtain up front, or their great linebackers. But it's time they start talking about a nifty secondary defense that's held together by Donnie Shell.

Although Shell had a sparkling college career at South Carolina State, the pros weren't even interested enough in 1974 to draft him. But Shell knocked on the Steeler's door and said, hey, look me over as a free agent. It cost the Steelers nothing but a plane ticket to take a look. They liked what they saw in camp and signed him.

The Steelers had been having a problem covering enemy tight ends who were fast and big. Shell had the speed and the courage to meet them head-on. He was in and out of the line-up mostly as a Special Teams player for three years and finally the Steelers had to admit he was not only good enough to stick around but to start. In 1977 he became a regular. Frankly, most of the teams in the NFL wondered why it took the Steelers so long to realize they had a budding star.

Last year the budding star burst into full bloom. Tough, quick, and smart, Shell was the glue that held the Steelers' secondary together as they roared to their fourth Super Bowl victory.

ALL-ROOKIE OFFENSE 1979

WR: **Jerry Butler**, Buffalo Bills
WR: **Earnest Gray**, New York Giants
 TE: **Dan Ross**, Cincinnati Bengals
  T: **Keith Dorney**, Detroit Lions
  T: **Dave Studdard**, Denver Broncos
  G: **Cody Risien**, Cleveland Browns
  G: **Greg Roberts**, Tampa Bay Buccaneers
  C: **Mark Dennard**, Miami Dolphins
QB: **Phil Simms**, New York Giants
RB: **Ottis Anderson**, St. Louis Cardinals
RB: **William Andrews**, Atlanta Falcons

JERRY BUTLER
6-0, 178
BUFFALO BILLS

Most NFL scouts said that Jerry Butler was the best college receiver in the country when he was a unanimous All-America at Clemson. His career stats showed 139 receptions for 2,223 yards and he had 58 of them as a senior.... Okay, said the critics, let's see him do it as a pro.... Whoooeee! Did Jerry Butler ever do it as a pro! He took his agile moves and his Atlantic Coast Conference 60-yard dash record into training camp.... And in a few days proved he belonged.... The Bills' QB, Joe Ferguson, soon was tickled Butler was around.... Butler was *all*-around as he put slick moves on NFL defenders for 48 receptions, 834 yards, and four touchdowns.... "Give this kid another year or two," said one veteran pro coach, "and you'll have to vote for him for All-Pro."

Wide Receiver
EARNEST GRAY
6-3, 195
NEW YORK GIANTS

If there's a faster wide receiver in the NFL than Earnie Gray, nobody knows who he is. This big blazer from Memphis State — a second-round draft choice— does the pro 40-yard test in 4.4.... He also  has the ability to change directions in high gear.... Add his glue-fingered mitts and you'll know why he had 97 career receptions for 2,123 yards in college—along with an eye-popping 21.9 yards average per catch.... The Giants gave him a quick shot at a starting position and Gray paid off.... The best defensive backs in the NFL had trouble covering him as he sped by them or faked them out of position.... And the stats tell a sweet story for this nifty receiver: 28 receptions for 537 yards, four touchdowns, and a brilliant 19.2 yards average per catch.

Tight End
DAN ROSS
6-4, 238
CINCINNATI BENGALS

Already they're comparing him with the Raiders' Dave Casper at the same stage of develop- ment .... And that's not a bad compari- son. ... This big, am- bitious rookie from Northeastern Uni- versity in Boston, picked up right where he left off in his college career where he caught 68 passes for 988 yards and seven TDs as a senior and made Little All- America (for colleges that aren't major football powers).... But the Bengals had scouted him well and drafted him in the second round.... They liked what the rest of the NFL agrees with now. ... Excellent size, great hands, quick, and fast enough to make the quick curl reception or go deep.... The Bengals' coaches wasted lit- tle time getting him into the line-up, where Ross, himself, wasted no time in learning how to cope with those smart de- fensive backs in the NFL. Those vet de- fenders had a hard time believing he was a newcomer.... In his first season he caught 41 passes for 516 yards.

Offensive Tackle
KEITH DORNEY
6-5, 265
DETROIT LIONS

The Lions knew what they were doing when they made Keith Dorney a first-round draft pick. ...Various scouting reports around the NFL described the Penn State All-America as: "A leader, intense, physical, tenacious, tough, and smart." Smart enough to also make Academic All-America as well as on the playing field. ... The Lions knew they were going to give Dorney a shot as starting tackle in pre-season camp and he disappointed nobody. ... Dorney made the transition from college ball to pro immediately. "Nothing was too tricky for him," says Detroit's head coach, Monte Clark. "We never had to tell him anything twice. He blasted out like a veteran pro. He hits like a truck. He could sustain a block and give pass protection. What else could we want?" The answer was "nothing." Other teams in the league soon wished Keith Dorney hadn't been so ready. Most of them predicted he'd be an All-Pro in three years or less.

DAVID STUDDARD

6-4, 255

DENVER BRONCOS

The Baltimore Colts wish they had a second chance with David Studdard. They drafted him out of the University of Texas in 1978 but whoever made decisions for the Colts weren't impressed by the rookie.... The Colts let him go and Denver took him on as a free-agent rookie for '79. What a take-on! The Broncos simply remembered that Studdard was the guy who cleared the biggest holes for Earl Campbell for three years. An All-Southwest Conference choice, Studdard exploded when he got his chance in the Broncos' pre-season camp. He was quick-footed and had excellent upper body strength. "We stuck him in there and the best defensive linemen in the NFL found they couldn't knock him off-balance or contain his charge," said Whitey Dovell, Broncos' offensive line coach. "I saw some of those opposing linemen shaking their heads after Studdard blocked him. "That's *respect*, man!"

Offensive Guard
CODY RISIEN
6-7, 255
CLEVELAND BROWNS

Cody Risien is the tallest guard in pro football history and his hopes for future All-Pro stardom are just as high....So you might as well know how to pronounce his name: "rise-un"....It took  Cody's teammates more time to learn this than it did for them to realize he was going to make the team....Risien, who received honorable mention All-America at Texas A&M, was only a seventh-round draft choice by the Browns but his quickness and fierce blocking soon had the coaches' attention....And given a chance to start, he caught the eye of defensive coaches throughout the NFL. They knew they wouldn't be able to out-smart or out-muscle THIS rookie .... A smart blocker and a cliff-high pass protector, it took him little time to show his star status.

Offensive Guard
GREG ROBERTS
6-3, 225
TAMPA BAY BUCCANEERS

Nobody down-grades Greg Roberts just because he was a second-round draft choice, and not a first. After all, he was the first offensive guard picked. ...And the Bucs couldn't wait to get their mitts on him .... They knew that Heisman Trophy winner Billy Sims had made some of his best yardage over Roberts' position at Oklahoma .... The Bucs also knew that Roberts had the size, strength, and quickness to open those kind of holes for their Ricky Bell, in the pros. ... The unanimous All-America was given the chance to prove he could do just that. In the Bucs' camp he adjusted quickly to pro-style blocking and immediately won a starting spot in the Buccaneer's line-up. Credit Roberts' rapid rise to stardom for much of Tampa's surge to the playoffs.

Center
MARK DENNARD
6-1, 250
MIAMI DOLPHINS

For years, Jim Langer had been an All-Pro standout at center for the Dolphins, but there had to come a day when he'd have to move aside for a younger man.... The younger guy at Miami is Mark Dennard, who looks as wide as a barn door, but don't try to drive through him. Dennard was only a tenth-round draft choice, and the 274th player chosen in 1978. When he broke a wrist in the preseason opener that year he was sidelined for the season. All things considered, Dennard's future didn't look promising — until he got another crack at a rookie season last year.... At Texas A&M, he was switched from guard to center as a sophomore and made All-Academic All-America.... The Dolphins liked his blocking and his hustle and gave him a chance to take the center position away from Langer. Enemy defenses DIDN'T like his blocking and hustle. Which is why he's All-Pro Rookie.

Phil Simms has the face of a choir boy and the right arm of a blacksmith, so don't let the face fool you.... The Giants' first-round draft pick played his college ball for little-known (football-wise) Morehead State in Kentucky because none of the biggies recruited him out of high school.... So Simms proved them all wrong with a collegiate career that showed him completing 409 passes in 836 attempts, for 5,545 yards.... The Giants checked him out and liked not only his arm but his coolness, poise, and some scrambling ability.... It didn't take the big blond very long to win the starting job with the Giants (it's rare for a QB to start as a rookie in the NFL).... By the season's end, he owned some glittering stats: 134 completions in 265 attempts for a nifty 50.6 percentage; 1,743 yards gained, and 13 touchdowns.... Now, if the Giants' offensive line can only give him a bit more protection Simms has a shot at real greatness.

OTTIS ANDERSON
6-1, 210
ST. LOUIS CARDINALS

(See All-Pro)

WILLIAM ANDREWS
6-0, 200
ATLANTA FALCONS

Rookie running backs who rush for 1,000 yards their first season are rare items. But William Andrews had an early start toward that magic mark.... As a high school star in Thomasville, Ga., he scampered for 4,339 yards and 60 touchdowns in three years. When he got to Auburn University the pattern was set. A brilliant future lay ahead after his sophomore year, but injuries kept cropping up.... Finally, in his senior season he was used mostly as a blocking back and only carried the ball 72 times....But Atlanta scouts had seen him shredding enemy defenses as a sophomore and junior. They weren't interested in a blocking back. They wanted Andrews for the green real estate he could cover.... The Falcons held their breath while other clubs passed him over in the first two draft rounds, and Atlanta grabbed him on the third.... What a grab it was. Andrews from early season on, sliced up some of the best defenses in the NFL.

59

ALL-ROOKIE DEFENSE 1979

E: **Dan Hampton**, Chicago Bears
E: **Jesse Baker**, Houston Oilers
T: **Manu Tuiasosopo**, Seattle Seahawks
T: **Fred Smerlas**, Buffalo Bills
LB: **Jerry Robinson**, Philadelphia Eagles
LB: **Stan Blinka**, New York Jets
LB: **Jim Haslett**, Buffalo Bills
CB: **Henry Williams**, Oakland Raiders
CB: **Larry Braziel**, Baltimore Colts
S: **Vernon Perry**, Houston Oilers
S: **Brenard Wilson**, Philadelphia Eagles

DAN HAMPTON
6-5, 256
CHICAGO BEARS

Dan Hampton's path to stardom was far from a usual one ....In the sixth grade, back on his family's farm in Arkansas, Dan broke both legs and an arm when he fell 45 feet from a tree he'd been climbing....In high school he was the biggest high school saxophone player in the state when a coach persuaded him to give up the sax and come out for football, instead....Hampton finally went along with the idea, became a high school All-America and an All-America at the University of Arkansas, where he was a starter all four years....The Bears made him a first-round draft choice and figured he could fit in at any of the four defensive line positions but decided to start him at tackle....After a week or so they saw his unusual speed and hand strength and knew they had a potential superstar at defensive end....NFL quarterbacks who dislike being sacked, wished he'd remained at tackle.

Defensive End
JESSE BAKER
6-4, 256
HOUSTON OILERS

When you're 6-4, weigh 256 pounds and can do 4.75 for the 40-yard dash, coaches start drooling in the NFL.... Baker, who starred at Jacksonville State in Alabama, just missed being a first-round draft choice but the Oilers quickly took him on the second round.... Houston scouts liked what they saw when Baker started in the '79 Senior Bowl game to wind up his brilliant college career.... Because of his strength, aggressiveness and quickness, teams had run away from his side in college, and the all-stars did the same.... In the Houston camp, Baker soon showed his potential....Veteran Oiler blockers thought they were hitting solid rock — but the rock could move, too.... When Baker started getting playing time during the regular season the word got around: "Here's a rookie you can't scare!" And soon it was Baker doing the scaring. Is there All-Pro in his future? Don't bet against it.

Defensive Tackle
MANU TUIASOSOPO
6-3, 252
SEATTLE SEAHAWKS

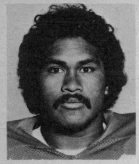

His full name is Man'ula Asovalu Tuiasosopo, which is a mouthful for fans and sports writers to deal with, but there was no problem at all back in the tiny island of Samoa in the South Pacific where he comes from... But when his family moved to Los Angeles he did the wise thing and shortened his first name to plain Manu and dropped the middle one.... Not many Samoans play football but UCLA recruited him for his tremendous strength and agility.... Manu was a terror for the Bruins and made second team All-America.... The Seahawks, tickled to get him in the first round of the draft, were even more so when they saw him tossing around the veterans in camp. An almost instant starter he was tabbed as a potential all-rookie before the season was half finished.... He's not the only Samoan in the NFL. He has three cousins in the league. QB Jack Thompson of the Cincinnati Bengals, Terry Tautolo, Philadelphia Eagles linebacker, and Frank Manumaleuga, Kansas City linebacker.

Defensive Tackle
FRED SMERLAS
6-3, 270
BUFFALO BILLS

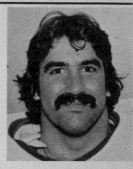

Although Boston College hadn't been making waves the last few years, pro scouts were among the most faithful spectators at the Eagles' games. The object of their attention was the Eagles' huge tackle who's been a fire-eating star for three years.... Although 270 pounds was a lot of weight for a guy only 6-3, the scouts knew he'd been New England heavyweight wrestling champ in high school and an All-American wrestler for BC.... Which meant he had great quickness and agility.... Tack that onto his strength and the Bills knew they'd be making no mistake in picking him as a second-round draft choice.... Smerlas impressed the Bills' coaches in camp and was just as effective at pro head-hunting when the season started.... NFL blockers found him difficult to move out and quarterbacks began to show great nervousness at the sight of the young monster bearing down on them with "sack" in his eye and mayhem in his heart....

Linebacker
STAN BLINKA
6-2, 230
NEW YORK JETS

When Stan Blinka is through with pro football he'd like to be a full-time rancher. If he's looking forward to steer-throwing contests he's getting a head start by throwing NFL ballcarriers for losses.... Only a fifth-round draft choice from Sam Houston State in Texas, he was considered a "good prospect" but nobody ever dreamed he'd come on so fast. Well, maybe Stan Blinka thought he would.... In pre-season camp he impressed Jet coaches with his quickness and great lateral pursuit — the natural gifts for a linebacker.... Once he nailed down a starting job, NFL offenses also found he had a nose for the ball and was always around it on running plays. Blockers found him hard to take out of a play and he seldom was fooled by the QB's faking...."A guy with a future," say NFL experts.

Linebacker
JIM HASLETT
6-3, 232
BUFFALO BILLS

He's from Indiana State. No, not from the biggie over in Hoosierland, but from little Indiana State in Pennsylvania....But the pros all knew about him, and the Bills considered themselves lucky when he was still available in the second round of the draft....Haslett led his college team in tackles his last two years and also handled the punting chores with a nifty 41.5 average....The Bills liked his quickness and his nose for the ball — and also knew he'd be very coachable because he'd been a quarterback in high school and picked up instructions quickly....Rival NFL teams found he was everything the Bills hoped he'd be — which means a pain-in-the-neck for enemy offenses....With defensive tackle rookie-star Fred Smerlas, he gives the Bills hope for the future.

Linebacker
JERRY ROBINSON
6-2, 216
PHILADELPHIA EAGLES

This was an easy choice to make.... Just as it was easy for the Eagles to make Robinson their first choice in the opening draft round.... At UCLA, Robinson had been recruited as a wide receiver by Dick Vermeil, then the UCLA coach, and now coach of the Eagles..., "He had tremendous speed," Vermeil recalls, "and we figured he'd catch passes all over the place, but then we found out he loved to hit and we shifted him to linebacker."...So Robinson became the first three-time All-American in UCLA history, with a career total of 480 tackles, most ever by a West Coast player....Reporting to the Eagles' camp he was an instant success and instant regular-season starter.... With his great speed he ran down fleet backs, shucked off blockers and sealed off the run, and batted down passes.... "If this guy is only a rookie," said one opposing coach, "think what he'll be in a couple of years!" Sure All-Pro, right?

67

HENRY WILLIAMS
5-10, 180
OAKLAND RAIDERS

Fans usually feel sorry for cornerbacks who come into the NFL at 5-10 and only 180 pounds. Little guys like that, say the fans, are going to get killed.... But don't waste any worry on Henry Wil-  liams.... They don't come any tougher or more fearless than the All-America from San Diego State in California.... But even though he was an All-America, the Raiders waited until the sixth round before tabbing Williams.... If he was going to have a size problem they'd find out about it soon enough in camp.... What the Raiders found out was that Williams hit like a 200-pounder, even when the biggest ball carriers or receivers came his way.... NFL opponents found out the same thing once the season began.... Like they say: "It isn't the size of the dog that counts in the fight; it's the size of the fight in the dog."

Cornerback
LARRY BRAZIEL
5-11, 193
BALTIMORE COLTS

When Larry Braziel reported to the Colts' training camp last summer, they listed him only number three at right cornerback. If he was going to play, he'd have to beat out two veterans. But it wasn't Mission Impossible for the former Southern California star. ... You learn to play tough and play smart as a Trojan, and Braziel didn't forget his tools when he reported to Baltimore .... The Colts' coaches soon did a lot of silent whistling and smiling among themselves as they watched Braziel cover talented veteran receivers and come up fast to nail hard-nosed runners at the line of scrimmage.... One of the toughest spots for a rookie to break in is at cornerback, but Braziel soon made enemy receivers and runners forget he was a newcomer...."Who does he think he is?" grumbled one opposing coach. Braziel thinks he is an All-Pro prospect some day.

Safety
VERNON PERRY
6-2, 211
HOUSTON OILERS

Vernon Perry was insulted. No team in the NFL thought enough of him to draft him. Okay, he'd sell his services on his own and knock a few heads off to prove he belonged. So he convinced the Oilers to take him on as a free agent and from Day One in camp he began drawing some rave reviews in staff meetings. ... Perry, who had starred four years for Jackson State in Mississippi, soon established himself as a starter—and why not? Look at the size that makes him one of the NFL's biggest defensive backs. ... Look at that speed and ability to take on the biggest, toughest tight ends. ... Look at those jarring hits he puts on receivers. ... And look at that attitude he had right from the start which says: "They can't insult *me*, man! This free agent is here to *play*!"

Safety
BRENARD WILSON
6-0, 170
PHILADELPHIA EAGLES

Brenard (no not Bernard) Wilson, doesn't let the odds get him down. Although he starred for three years at Vanderbilt, the Eagles weren't very high on him. They drafted him in a low round in 1978.... The Eagles took a look in training camp and weren't too impressed. They cut him, but a year later Wilson came around and said, okay, take another look at me as a free agent. No charge. Costs you nothing. The Eagles took a second look and quickly decided they'd made a serious mistake a year earlier.... Wilson not only stayed on but won a starting job with his hard-hitting, and nose for the ball.... One of the lightest safeties in the NFL at only 170 pounds, it never bothered him when he had to cover and bring down tight ends who outweighed him by 70 pounds. "The guy is all heart," said one admiring NFL coach. "Get yourself a few like that and you win a championship."

71

1979 FINAL STANDINGS
AMERICAN FOOTBALL
CONFERENCE

EASTERN DIVISION

	W	L	T	Pct.	Pts.	OP
* Miami	10	6	0	.625	341	257
New England	9	7	0	.563	411	326
N.Y. Jets	8	8	0	.500	337	383
Buffalo	7	9	0	.438	268	279
Baltimore	5	11	0	.313	271	351

CENTRAL DIVISION

	W	L	T	Pct.	Pts.	OP
* Pittsburgh	12	4	0	.750	416	262
#Houston	11	5	0	.688	362	331
Cleveland	9	7	0	.563	359	352
Cincinnati	4	12	0	.250	337	421

WESTERN DIVISION

	W	L	T	Pct.	Pts.	OP
* San Diego	12	4	0	.750	411	246
#Denver	10	6	0	.625	289	262
Seattle	9	7	0	.563	378	372
Oakland	9	7	0	.563	365	337
Kansas City	7	9	0	.438	238	262

*Division Champion
#Wild Card For Playoffs

AFC PLAYOFFS
AFC First Round
Houston 13, Denver 7
Divisional Playoffs
Houston 17, San Diego 14
Pittsburgh 34, Miami 14
Championship Game
Pittsburgh 27, Houston 13
Super Bowl XIV
Pittsburgh 31, Los Angeles 19

...And Previews for 1980 $\longrightarrow$

New England Patriots

Steve Grogan...The PATS must depend on the QB for a comeback.

QUARTERBACKING:	
RUNNING:	
RECEIVING:	
OFFENSIVE LINE:	
DEFENSE:	

Miami Dolphins

Nat Moore...One of the niftiest receivers in all of football.

QUARTERBACKING:	
RUNNING:	
RECEIVING:	
OFFENSIVE LINE:	
DEFENSE:	

73

Baltimore Colts

Joe Washington...Best combination runner, receiver in the league.

QUARTERBACKING:
RUNNING:
RECEIVING:
OFFENSIVE LINE:
DEFENSE:

New York Jets

Richard Todd...QB will throw to fastest receivers in the NFL.

QUARTERBACKING:
RUNNING:
RECEIVING:
OFFENSIVE LINE:
DEFENSE:

Buffalo Bills

Joe Ferguson...Bills' hopes, if any, ride on QB's right arm.

QUARTERBACKING: 🏈🏈🏈🏈
RUNNING: 🏈🏈🏈🏈
RECEIVING: 🏈🏈🏈🏈
OFFENSIVE LINE: 🏈🏈🏈🏈
DEFENSE: 🏈🏈🏈🏈

WESTERN DIVISION

San Diego Chargers

Clarence Williams...His running sets things up for Fouts' passes.

QUARTERBACKING: 🏈🏈🏈🏈🏈
RUNNING: 🏈🏈🏈
RECEIVING: 🏈🏈🏈🏈
OFFENSIVE LINE: 🏈🏈🏈🏈
DEFENSE: 🏈🏈🏈🏈

Oakland Raiders

Dan Pastorini...Raiders got top QB in trade with Houston Oilers

QUARTERBACKING: ⬤ ⬤ ⬤ ⬤
RUNNING: ⬤ ⬤ ⬤ ⬤
RECEIVING: ⬤ ⬤ ⬤ ⬤
OFFENSIVE LINE: ⬤ ⬤ ⬤ ◖
DEFENSE: ⬤ ⬤ ⬤ ◖

Denver Broncos

Haven Moses...Great receiver hauls in spectacular catches.

QUARTERBACKING: ⬤ ⬤ ⬤ ◖
RUNNING: ⬤ ⬤ ⬤ ⬤
RECEIVING: ⬤ ⬤ ⬤ ◖
OFFENSIVE LINE: ⬤ ⬤ ⬤ ⬤
DEFENSE: ⬤ ⬤ ⬤ ⬤

Seattle Seahawks

Steve Largent...Ace receiver for Zorn's zippy aerials.

QUARTERBACKING:
RUNNING:
RECEIVING:
OFFENSIVE LINE:
DEFENSE:

Kansas City Chiefs

Ted McKnight...He's the workhorse of the Chiefs' running game.

QUARTERBACKING:
RUNNING:
RECEIVING:
OFFENSIVE LINE:
DEFENSE:

Pittsburgh Steelers

Terry Bradshaw...Ace QB predicts another Super Bowl win.

QUARTERBACKING:	
RUNNING:	
RECEIVING:	
OFFENSIVE LINE:	
DEFENSE:	

Houston Oilers

Rob Carpenter...Helps Earl Campbell carry the running load.

QUARTERBACKING:	
RUNNING:	
RECEIVING:	
OFFENSIVE LINE:	
DEFENSE:	

Cincinnati Bengals

Ken Anderson...Nifty QB needs better blocking up front.

QUARTERBACKING:
RUNNING:
RECEIVING:
OFFENSIVE LINE:
DEFENSE:

Cleveland Browns

Mike Pruitt...Major part of Browns' ground attack.

QUARTERBACKING:
RUNNING:
RECEIVING:
OFFENSIVE LINE:
DEFENSE:

1979 FINAL STANDINGS NATIONAL FOOTBALL CONFERENCE

EASTERN DIVISION

	W	L	T	Pct.	Pts.	OP
* Dallas	11	5	0	.688	371	313
# Philadelphia	11	5	0	.688	339	282
Washington	10	6	0	.625	348	295
N.Y. Giants	6	10	0	.375	237	323
St. Louis	5	11	0	.313	307	358

CENTRAL DIVISION

	W	L	T	Pct.	Pts.	OP
* Tampa Bay	10	6	0	.625	273	237
# Chicago	10	6	0	.625	306	249
Minnesota	7	9	0	.438	259	337
Green Bay	5	11	0	.313	246	316
Dtroit	2	14	0	.125	219	365

WESTERN DIVISION

	W	L	T	Pct.	Pts.	OP
* Los Angeles	9	7	0	.563	323	309
New Orleans	8	8	0	.500	370	360
Atlanta	6	10	0	.375	300	388
San Francisco	2	14	0	.125	308	416

*Division Champion
#Wild Card for Playoffs

NFC Playoffs
NFC First Round
Philadelphia 27, Chicago 17
NFC Divisional Playoffs
Tampa Bay 24, Philadelphia 17
Los Angeles 21, Dallas 19
NFC Championship Game
Los Angeles 9, Tampa Bay 0
Super Bowl XIV
Pittsburgh 31, Los Angeles 19

...And Previews for 1980 ⟶

Philadelphia Eagles

Harold Carmichael...The 6-8 receiver is big touchdown threat.

QUARTERBACKING: 🏈 🏈 🏈 ◖
RUNNING: 🏈 🏈 🏈
RECEIVING: 🏈 🏈 🏈
OFFENSIVE LINE: 🏈 🏈 🏈 ◖
DEFENSE: 🏈 🏈 🏈

Dallas Cowboys

Tony Dorsett...With Staubach gone, his running is main threat.

QUARTERBACKING: 🏈 🏈 🏈
RUNNING: 🏈 🏈 🏈 ◖
RECEIVING: 🏈 🏈 🏈 ◖
OFFENSIVE LINE: 🏈 🏈 🏈 🏈
DEFENSE: 🏈 🏈 🏈 🏈 ◖

New York Giants

Brad Van Pelt...Year after year, a linebacking star.

QUARTERBACKING:	
RUNNING:	
RECEIVING:	
OFFENSIVE LINE:	
DEFENSE:	

Washington Redskins

Joe Theismann...Never an All-Pro QB but he gets the job done.

QUARTERBACKING:
RUNNING:
RECEIVING:
OFFENSIVE LINE:
DEFENSE:

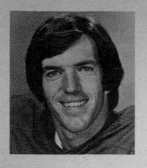

St. Louis Cardinals

Roger Wehrli...Former All-Pro cornerback still does the job.

QUARTERBACKING:	⬬	⬬	⬬	⬬
RUNNING:	⬬	⬬	⬬	◖
RECEIVING:	⬬	⬬	⬬	◖
OFFENSIVE LINE:	⬬	⬬	⬬	⬬
DEFENSE:	⬬	⬬	◖	

Los Angeles Rams

Bob Brudzinski...The rangy linebacker is a born defender.

QUARTERBACKING:	⬬	⬬	⬬	◖
RUNNING:	⬬	⬬	⬬	⬬
RECEIVING:	⬬	⬬	⬬	⬬
OFFENSIVE LINE:	⬬	⬬	⬬	⬬
DEFENSE:	⬬	⬬	⬬	⬬

Atlanta Falcons

Warren Bryant...Solid tackle in Falcons' offensive line.

QUARTERBACKING: 🏈 🏈 🏈 ◖
RUNNING: 🏈 🏈 🏈
RECEIVING: 🏈 🏈 ◖
OFFENSIVE LINE: 🏈 🏈 🏈 ◖
DEFENSE: 🏈 🏈 🏈 🏈

San Francisco 49ers

Steve DeBerg...Ace QB had a brilliant .600 pct. a year ago.

QUARTERBACKING: 🏈 🏈 🏈
RUNNING: 🏈 🏈
RECEIVING: 🏈 🏈 🏈 ◖
OFFENSIVE LINE: 🏈 🏈 🏈 ◖
DEFENSE: 🏈 🏈 🏈 ◖

New Orleans Saints

Chuck Muncie...This running back is one of league's best.

QUARTERBACKING: 🏈 🏈 🏈 🏈
RUNNING: 🏈 🏈 🏈 ◖
RECEIVING: 🏈 🏈 🏈 ◖
OFFENSIVE LINE: 🏈 🏈 🏈
DEFENSE: 🏈 🏈 🏈 ◖

CENTRAL DIVISION

Tampa Bay Buccaneers

David Lewis...Tough linebacker was an All-NFC selection in '79.

QUARTERBACKING: 🏈 🏈 🏈 🏈
RUNNING: 🏈 🏈 🏈
RECEIVING: 🏈 🏈 🏈
OFFENSIVE LINE: 🏈 🏈 🏈 ◖
DEFENSE: 🏈 🏈 🏈 🏈

Chicago Bears

Walter Payton...One of NFL's all-time great ball carriers.

QUARTERBACKING:
RUNNING:
RECEIVING:
OFFENSIVE LINE:
DEFENSE:

Minnesota Vikings

Ahmad Rashad...Slick receiver may be the best in the league.

QUARTERBACKING:
RUNNING:
RECEIVING:
OFFENSIVE LINE:
DEFENSE:

Green Bay Packers

Johnnie Gray...Fine defensive back is team's top interceptor.

QUARTERBACKING: 🏈 🏈 🏈
RUNNING: 🏈 🏈 🏈
RECEIVING: 🏈 🏈 🏈
OFFENSIVE LINE: 🏈 🏈 🏈
DEFENSE: 🏈 🏈 🏈 ◗

Detroit Lions

Freddie Scott...Fleet wide receiver caught 62 passes in '79.

QUARTERBACKING: 🏈 🏈 🏈 ◗
RUNNING: 🏈 🏈 🏈 ◗
RECEIVING: 🏈 🏈 🏈 ◗
OFFENSIVE LINE: 🏈 🏈 🏈 ◗
DEFENSE: 🏈 🏈 🏈 ◗

HOW THEY'RE PICKED
TO FINISH IN 1980

AFC

East	West	Central
1. New England	1. San Diego	1. Pittsburgh
2. Miami	2. Oakland	2. Houston
3. Baltimore	3. Denver	3. Cincinnati
4. New York Jets	4. Seattle	4. Cleveland
5. Buffalo	5. Kansas City	

NFC

East	West	Central
1. Philadelphia	1. Los Angeles	1. Tampa Bay
2. Dallas	2. Atlanta	2. Chicago
3. New York Giants	3. San Francisco	3. Minnesota
4. Washington	4. New Orleans	4. Green Bay
5. St. Louis		5. Detroit

Super Bowl XV
Pittsburgh vs. Los Angeles

Best Bet for
Rookie-of-the-Year
Billy Sims, Detroit Lions

1979 RECORDS

SCORING

POINTS
    Kickers
AFC: 115 John Smith, New England
NFC: 114 Mark Moseley, Washington
    Non-kickers
AFC: 114 Earl Campbell, Houston
NFC: 96 Walter Payton, Chicago

TOUCHDOWNS
AFC: 19 Earl Campbell, Houston (19 rushing)
NFC: 16 Walter Payton, Chicago (14 rushing, 2 receiving)

EXTRA POINTS
AFC: 50 Matt Bahr, Pittsburgh (52 attempts)
NFC: 40 Rafael Septien, Dallas (44 attempts)

FIELD GOALS
NFC: 25 Mark Moseley, Washington (33 attempts)
AFC: 23 John Smith, New England (33 attempts)

MOST POINTS, GAME
AFC: 24 points Jerry Butler, Buffalo vs. New York Jets,
    September 23 (4TDs)
Roland Hooks, Buffalo vs. Cincinnati, September 9 (4 TDs)
Clarence Williams, San Diego vs. Buffalo, September 16 (4 TDs)
NFC: 24 points Wilbert Montgomery, Philadelphia vs.
    Washington, October 7 (4 TDs)
Ahmad Rashad, Minnesota vs. San Francisco, September 2 (4 TDs)

TEAM LEADERS

AFC: BALTIMORE: 61, Steve Mike-Mayer; BUFFALO: 77, Nick Mike-Mayer; CINCINNATI: 90, Pete Johnson; CLEVELAND: 89, Don Cockroft; DENVER: 71, Jim Turner; HOUSTON: 114, Earl Campbell; KANSAS CITY: 64, Jan Stenerud; MIAMI: 99, Uwe von Schamann; NEW ENGLAND: 115, John Smith; NEW YORK JETS: 42, Kevin Long; OAKLAND: 95, Jim Breech; PITTSBURGH: 104, Matt Bahr; SAN DIEGO: 72, Clarence Williams; SEATTLE:100 Efren Herrera.

NFC: ATLANTA: 70, Tim Mazzetti; CHICAGO: 96, Walter Payton; DALLAS: 97, Rafael Septien; DETROIT: 55, Benny Ricardo; GREEN BAY: 28, Tom Birney & Chester Marcol; LOS ANGELES: 75, Frank Corral; MINNESOTA: 67, Rick Danmeier; NEW ORLEANS: 75, Garo Yepremian; NEW YORK GIANTS: 66, Billy Taylor; PHILADELPHIA: 105, Tony Franklin; ST LOUIS: 60, Ottis Anderson; SAN FRANCISCO: 92, Ray Wersching; TAMPA BAY: 63, Neil O'Donoghue; WASHINGTON: 114, Mark Moseley.

TEAM CHAMPION

AFC: 416 Pittsburgh
NFC: 371 Dallas

TOP TEN SCORERS — NON-KICKERS

	TD	R	P	M	PTS
Campbell, Earl, Hou.	19	19	0	0	114
Payton, Walter, Chi.	16	14	2	0	96
Johnson, Pete, Cin.	15	14	1	0	90
Smith, Sherman, Sea.	15	11	4	0	90
Montgomery, Wilbert, Phil.	14	9	5	0	84
Csonka, Larry, Mia.	13	12	1	0	78
Morgan, Stanley, N.E.	13	0	12	1	78
Harris, Franco, Pitt.	12	11	1	0	72
Riggins, John, Wash.	12	9	3	0	72
Williams, Clarence, S.D.	12	12	0	0	72

TOP TEN SCORERS — KICKERS

	XP	XPA	FG	FGA	PTS
Smith, John, N.E.	46	49	23	33	115
Moseley, Mark, Wash.	39	39	25	33	114
Franklin, Tony, Phil. . . . . . . ,	36	39	23	31	105
Bahr, Matt, Pitt.	50	52	18	30	104
Fritsch, Toni, Hou.	41	43	21	25	104
Herrera, Efren, Sea.	43	46	19	23	100
von Schamann, Uwe, Mia. . . .	36	40	21	29	99
Septien, Rafael, Dall.	40	44	19	29	97
Breech, Jim, Oak.	41	45	18	27	95
Wersching, Ray, S.F.	32	35	20	24	92

AFC — INDIVIDUALS

NON-KICKERS

	TD	R	P	M	PTS
Campbell, Earl, Hou. . . . . . . :	19	19	0	0	114
Johnson, Pete, Cin.	15	14	1	0	90
Smith, Sherman, Sea.	15	11	4	0	90
Csonka, Larry, Mia.	13	12	1	0	78
Morgan, Stenley, N.E.	13	0	12	1	78
Harris, Franco, Pitt.	12	11	1	0	72
Williams, Clarence, S.D.	12	12	0	0	72
Pruitt, Mike, Clev.	11	9	2	0	66
Jefferson, John, S.D.	10	0	10	0	60
Thornton, Sidney, Pitt.	10	6	4	0	60

NFC — INDIVIDUALS

NON-KICKERS

	TD	R	P	M	PTS
Payton, Walter, Chi.	16	14	2	0	96
Montgomery, Wilbert, Phil. . .	14	9	5	0	84

Riggins, John, Wash.	12	9	3	0	72
Carmichael, Harold, Phil.	11	0	11	0	66
Muncie, Chuck, N.O.	11	11	0	0	66
Taylor, Billy, N.Y.G.	11	7	4	0	66
Anderson, Ottis, St. L.	10	8	2	0	60
Galbreath, Tony, N.O.	10	9	1	0	#60
Hill, Tony, Dall.	10	0	10	0	60
Tyler, Wendell, L.A.	10	9	1	0	60

RUSHING

YARDS
AFC: 1967 Earl Campbell, Houston
NFC: 1610 Walter Payton, Chicago

YARDS PER ATTEMPT
NFC: 5.1 Wendell Tyler, Los Angeles
AFC: 5.0 Sidney Thornton, Pittsburgh

TOUCHDOWNS
AFC: 19 Earl Campbell, Houston
NFC: 14 Walter Payton, Chicago

ATTEMPTS
NFC: 369 Walter Payton, Chicago
AFC: 368 Earl Campbell, Houston

LONGEST
AFC: 84 yards Ted McKnight, Kansas City vs. Seattle, September 30 (TD)
NFC: 80 yards Leroy Harris, Philadelphia vs. Green Bay, November 25

MOST YARDS, GAME

NFC: 197 yards (30 attempts)   Wilbert Montgomery, Philadelphia
vs. Cleveland, November 4

AFC: 195 yards (33 attempts)   Earl Campbell, Houston vs. Dallas,
November 22

TEAM LEADERS

AFC: BALTIMORE: 884, Joe Washington; BUFFALO: 574, Curtis
Brown; CINCINNATI: 865, Pete Johnson; CLEVELAND: 1294,
Mike Pruitt; DENVER: 453, Otis Armstrong; HOUSTON: 1967,
Earl Campbell; KANSAS CITY: 755, Ted McKnight; MIAMI: 837,
Larry Csonka; NEW ENGLAND: 563, Sam Cunningham; NEW
YORK JETS: 905, Clark Gaines; OAKLAND: 818, Mark van
Eeghen; PITTSBURGH: 1186, Franco Harris; SAN DIEGO: 752,
Clarence Williams; SEATTLE: 775, Sherman Smith.

NFC: ATLANTA: 1023, William Andrews; CHICAGO: 1610, Walter
Payton; DALLAS: 1107, Tony Dorsett, DETROIT: 625, Dexter
Bussey; GREEN BAY: 495, Terdell Middleton; LOS ANGELES:
1109, Wendell Tyler; MINNESOTA: 708, Rickey Young; NEW
ORLEANS: 1198, Chuck Muncie; NEW YORK GIANTS: 700, Billy
Taylor; PHILADELPHIA: 1512, Wilbert Montgomery; ST. LOUIS:
1605, Ottis Anderson; SAN FRANCISCO: 615, Paul Hofer; TAMPA
BAY: 1263, Ricky Bell; WASHINGTON: 1153, John Riggins.

TEAM CHAMPION

AFC: 2646   New York Jets
NFC: 2582   St. Louis

TOP TEN RUSHERS

	Att	Yards	Avg	Long	TD
Campbell, Earl, Hou.	368	1697	4.6	t61	19
Payton, Walter, Chi.	369	1610	4.4	t43	14
Anderson, Ottis, St. L.	331	1605	4.8	t76	8
Montgomery, Wilbert, Phil.	338	1512	4.5	t62	9

	Att	Yards	Avg	Long	TD
Pruitt, Mike, Clev.	264	1294	4.9	t77	9
Bell, Ricky, T.B.	283	1263	4.5	49	7
Muncie, Chuck, N.O.	238	1198	5.0	t69	11
Harris, Franco, Pitt.	267	1186	4.4	t71	11
Riggins, John, Wash.	260	1153	4.4	t66	9
Tyler, Wendell, L.A. ....·	218	1109	5.1	t63	9

AFC — INDIVIDUALS

	Att	Yards	Avg	Long	TD
Campbell, Earl, Hou.	368	1697	4.6	t61	19
Pruitt, Mike, Clev. .,.......	264	1294	4.9	t77	9
Harris, Franco, Pitt.	267	1186	4.4	t71	11
Gaines, Clark, N.Y.J.	186	905	4.9	52	0
Washington, Joe, Balt.	242	884	3.7	26	4
Johnson, Pete, Cin.	243	865	3.6	t35	14
Csonka, Larry, Mia.	220	837	3.8	22	12
van Eeghan, Mark, Oak. .....:	223	818	3.7	19	7
Smith, Sherman, Sea.	194	775	4.0	31	11
Dierking, Scott, N.Y.J.	186	767	4.1	40	3
McKnight, Ted, K.C.	153	755	4.9	t84	8
Williams, Clarence, S.D.	200	752	3.8	t55	12
Williams, Delvin, Mia.	184	703	3.8	39	3
Griffin, Archie, Cin.	140	688	4.9	63	0
Thornton, Sidney, Pitt.	118	585	5.0	75	6

NFC — INDIVIDUALS

	Att	Yards	Avg	Long	TD
Payton, Walter, Chi.	369	1610	4.4	t43	14
Anderson, Ottis, St. L.	331	1605	4.8	t76	8
Montgomery, Wilbert, Phil. ..	338	1512	4.5	t62	9
Bell, Ricky, T.B.	283	1263	4.5	49	7
Muncie, Chuck, N.O.	238	1198	5.0	t69	11

Riggins, John, Wash.	260	1153	4.4	t66	9
Tyler, Wendell, L.A.	218	1109	5.1	t63	9
Dorsett, Tony, Dall.	250	1107	4.4	41	6
Andrews, William, Atl.	239	1023	4.3	23	3
Young, Rickey, Minn.	188	708	3.8	26	3
Galbreath, Tony, N.O.	189	708	3.7	27	9
Taylor, Billy, N.Y.G.	198	700	3.5	31	7
Eckwood, Jerry, T.B.	194	690	3.6	t61	2
Bussey, Dexter, Det.	144	625	4.3	38	1
Bryant, Cullen, L.A.	177	619	3.5	15	5

PASSING

HIGHEST RATING
NFC: 92.4 Roger Staubach, Dallas
AFC: 82.6 Dan Fouts, San Diego

ATTEMPTS
NFC: 578 Steve DeBerg, San Francisco
AFC: 535 Brian Sipe, Cleveland

COMPLETIONS
NFC: 347 Steve DeBerg, San Francisco
AFC: 332 Dan Fouts, San Diego

COMPLETION PERCENTAGE
AFC: 62.6 Dan Fouts, San Diego (530 attempts, 332
    completions)
NFC: 60.0 Steve DeBerg, San Francisco (578 attempts, 347
    completions)

YARDS
AFC: 4082 Dan Fouts, San Diego
NFC: 3652 Steve DeBerg, San Francisco

TOUCHDOWN PASSES
AFC: 28 Steve Grogan, New England
Brian Sipe, Cleveland
NFC: 27 Roger Staubach, Dallas

INTERCEPTIONS
AFC: 26 Brian Sipe, Cleveland
NFC: 24 Tommy Kramer, Minnesota
Doug Williams, Tampa Bay

LOWEST PERCENTAGE INTERCEPTED
NFC: 2.4 Roger Staubach, Dallas (461 attempts, 11 intercepted)
AFC: 2.9 Ken Anderson, Cincinnati (339 attempts, 10 intercepted)

TEAM CHAMPION
NFC: 90.3 Dallas
AFC: 81.6 Oakland

TOP TEN INDIVIDUAL PASSING QUALIFIERS

	Att	Comp	Yards	TD	Int	Rating Points
Staubach, Roger, Dall.	461	267	3586	27	11	92.4
Theismann, Joe, Wash.	395	233	2797	20	13	84.0
Fouts, Dan, S.D.	530	332	4082	24	24	82.6
Stabler, Ken, Oak.	498	304	3615	26	22	82.2
Anderson, Ken, Cin.	339	189	2340	16	10	80.9
Zorn, Jim, Sea.	505	285	3361	20	18	77.6
Grogan, Steve, N.E.	423	206	3286	28	20	77.5
Bradshaw, Terry, Pitt.	472	259	3724	26	25	77.0
Jaworski, Ron, Phil.	374	190	2669	18	12	76.8
Manning, Archie, N.O.	420	252	3169	15	20	75.6

AFC INDIVIDUAL QUALIFIERS

	Att	Comp	Yards	TD	Int	Rating Points
Fouts, Dan, S.D.	530	332	4082	24	24	82.6
Stabler, Ken, Oak.	498	304	3615	26	22	82.2
Anderson, Ken, Cin.	339	189	2340	16	10	80.9
Zorn, Jim, Sea.	505	285	3661	20	18	77.6
Grogan, Steve, N.E.	423	206	3286	28	20	77.5
Bradshaw, Terry, Pitt.	472	259	3724	26	25	77.0
Landry, Greg, Balt.	457	270	2932	15	15	75.3
Ferguson, Joe, Buff.	458	238	3572	14	15	74.5
Sipe, Brian, Clev.	535	286	3793	28	26	73.1
Griese, Bob, Mia.	310	176	2160	14	16	71.8
Morton, Craig, Den.	370	204	2626	16	19	70.7
Todd, Richard, N.Y.J.	334	171	2660	16	22	66.4
Pastorini, Dan, Hou.	324	163	2090	14	18	61.9
Fuller, Steve, K.C.	270	146	1484	6	14	55.8

NFC INDIVIDUAL QUALIFIERS

	Att	Comp	Yards	TD	Int	Rating Points
Staubach, Roger, Dall.	461	267	3586	27	11	92.4
Theismann, Joe, Wash.	395	233	2797	20	13	84.0
Jaworski, Ron, Phil.	374	190	2669	18	12	76.8
Manning, Archie, N.O.	420	252	3169	15	20	75.6
DeBerg, Steve, S.F.	578	347	3652	17	21	73.1
Kramer, Tommy, Minn.	566	315	3397	23	24	69.7
Phipps, Mike, Chi.	255	134	1535	9	8	69.7
Haden, Pat, L.A.	290	163	1854	11	14	68.2
Bartowski, Steve, Atl.	380	204	2505	17	20	67.2
Simms, Phil, N.Y.G.	265	134	1743	13	14	65.9
Whitehurst, David, G.B.	322	179	2247	10	18	64.5
Hart, Jim, St. L.	378	194	2218	9	20	55.2
Williams, Doug, T.B.	397	166	2448	18	24	52.6
Komlo, Jeff, Det.	368	183	2238	11	23	52.6

PASS RECEIVING

RECEPTIONS
AFC: 82 Joe Washington, Baltimore
NFC: 80 Ahmad Rashad, Minnesota

YARDS
AFC: 1237 Steve Largent, Seattle
NFC: 1156 Ahmad Rashad, Minnestoa

YARDS PER RECEPTION
AFC: 22.8 Stanley Morgan, New England (44 receptions, 1002 yards)
NFC: 18.7 Drew Pearson, Dallas (55 receptions, 1026 yards)

TOUCHDOWNS
AFC: 12 Stanley Morgan, New England
NFC: 11 Harold Carmichael, Philadelphia

LONGEST
NFC: 85 yards Wes Chandler, New Orleans vs. San Francisco, September 23 (from Archie Manning)
AFC: 84 yards Curtis Brown, Buffalo vs. San Diego, September 16 (from Joe Ferguson) — TD

MOST RECEPTIONS, GAME
NFC: 15 (116 yards) Rickey Young, Minnesota vs. New England, December 16
AFC: 13 (130 yards) Joe Washington, Baltimore vs. Kansas City, September 2

TEAM LEADERS
AFC: BALTIMORE: 82, Joe Washington; BUFFALO: 54, Frank Lewis; CINCINNATI: 58, Don Bass; CLEVELAND: 59, Dave Logan; DENVER: 64, Rick Upchurch; HOUSTON: 40, Ken Burrough; KANSAS CITY: 38, Ted McKnight; MIAMI: 48, Nat Moore; NEW

98

ENGLAND: 45, Harold Jackson; NEW YORK JETS: 32, Derrick Gaffney; OAKLAND: 59, Cliff Branch; PITTSBURGH: 70, John Stallworth; SAN DIEGO: 72, Charlie Joiner; SEATTLE: 66, Steve Largent.

NFC: ATLANTA: 74, Wallace Francis; CHICAGO: 42, David Williams; DALLAS: 60, Tony Hill; DETROIT: 62, Freddie Scott; GREEN BAY: 56, Paul Coffman; LOS ANGELES: 43, Preston Dennard; MINNESOTA: 80, Ahmad Rashad; NEW ORLEANS: 65, Wes Chandler; NEW YORK GIANTS: 31, Gary Shirk; PHILADELPHIA: 52, Harold Carmichael; ST. LOUIS: 57, Pat Tilley; SAN FRANCISCO: 58, Paul Hofer; TAMPA BAY: 40, Jimmie Giles; WASHINGTON: 46, Danny Buggs.

TOP TEN PASS RECEIVERS

	No	Yards	Avg	Long	TD
Washington, Joe, Balt.	82	750	9.1	t43	3
Rashad, Ahmad, Minn.	80	1156	14.5	t52	9
Francis, Wallace, Atl.	74	1013	13.7	42	8
Joiner, Charlie, S.D.	72	1008	14.0	39	4
Young, Rickey, Minn.	72	519	7.2	18	4
Stallworth, John, Pitt.	70	1183	16.9	t65	8
Largent, Steve, Sea.	66	1237	18.7	t55	9
Chandler, Wes, N.O.	65	1069	16.4	85	6
Upchurch, Rick, Den.	64	937	14.6	47	7
Scott, Freddie, Det.	62	929	15.0	50	5

AFC — INDIVIDUALS

	No	Yards	Avg	Long	TD
Washington, Joe, Balt.	82	750	9.1	t43	3
Joiner, Charlie, S.D.	72	1008	14.0	39	4
Stallworth, John, Pitt.	70	1183	16.9	t65	8
Largent, Steve, Sea.	66	1237	18.7	t55	9
Upchurch, Rick, Den.	64	937	14.6	47	7

Jefferson, John, S.D.	61	1090	17.9	t65	10
Logan, Dave, Clev.	59	982	16.6	46	7
Branch, Cliff, Oak.	59	844	14.3	t66	6
Bass, Don, Cin.	58	724	12.5	50	3
Chester, Raymond, Oak.	58	712	12.3	39	8
Casper, Dave, Oak.	57	771	13.5	42	3
Newsome, Ozzie, Clev.	55	781	14.2	74	9
McCauley, Don, Balt.	55	575	10.5	35	3
Lewis, Frank, Buff.	54	1082	20.0	55	2
Moses, Haven, Den.	54	943	17.5	t64	6

NFC — INDIVIDUALS

	No	Yards	Avg	Long	TD
Rashad, Ahmad, Minn.	80	1156	14.5	t52	9
Francis, Wallace, Atl.	74	1013	13.7	42	8
Young, Rickey, Minn.	72	519	7.2	18	4
Chandler, Wes, N.O.	65	1069	16.4	85	6
Scott, Freddie, Det.	62	929	15.0	50	5
Hill, Tony, Dall.	60	1062*	17.7	t75	10
Hofer, Paul, S.F.	58	662	11.4	44	2
Galbreath, Tony, N.O.	58	484	8.3	38	1
Tilley, Pat, St. L.	57	938	16.5	t51	6
Solomon, Freddie, S.F.	57	807	14.2	t44	7
Coffman, Paul, G.B.	56	711	12.7	t78	4
Pearson, Drew, Dall.	55	1026	18.7	t56	8
Lofton, James, G.B.	54	968	17.9	52	4
Jackson, Wilbur, S.F.	53	422	8.0	34	0
Carmichael, Harold, Phil.	52	872	16.8	50	11

INTERCEPTIONS

INTERCEPTIONS
AFC: 12 Mike Reinfeldt, Houston
NFC: 9 Lemar Parrish, Washington

YARDS
AFC: 205 Mike Reinfeldt, Houston
NFC: 127 Tom Myers, New Orleans

TOUCHDOWNS
AFC: 2 Lester Hayes, Oakland
        Woodrow Lowe, San Diego
NFC: 2 Jim Youngblood, Los Angeles

LONGEST
NFC: 96 yards Ray Griffin, Cincinnati vs. San Diego, November 11 (TD)
AFC: 78 yards Carl Allen, St. Louis vs. Chicago, December 16

TEAM LEADERS
AFC: BALTIMORE: 4, Lyle Blackwood, Larry Braziel & Sanders Shiver; BUFFALO: 6, Jeff Nixon; CINCINNATI: 6, Dick Jauron; CLEVELAND: 5, Thom Darden; DENVER: 6, Steve Foley; HOUSTON: 12, Mike Reinfeldt; KANSAS CITY: 7, Gary Barbaro; MIAMI: 5, Neal Colzie & Gerald Small; NEW ENGLAND: 5, Raymond Clayborn; NEW YORK JETS: 6, Burgess Owens; OAKLAND: 7, Lester Hayes; PITTSBURGH: 6, Jack Lambert; SAN DIEGO: 5, Woodrow Lowe & Ray Preston: SEATTLE: 5, Dave Brown.

NFC: ATLANTA: 6, Rolland Lawrence; CHICAGO: 6, Gary Fencik & Terry Schmidt; DALLAS: 2, five players; DETROIT: 4, Jimmy Allen & Luther Bradley; GREEN BAY: 5, Johnnie Gray; LOS ANGELES: 5, Nolan Cromwell & Jim Youngblood; MINNESOTA: 4, Tom Hannon & Nate Wright; NEW ORLEANS: 7, Tom Myers; NEW YORK GIANTS: 3, Harry Carson, Terry Jackson & Brian kelley; PHILADELPHIA: 4, Brenard Wilson; ST. LOUIS: 6, Ken Stone; SAN FRANCISCO: 5, Dwight Hicks; TAMPA BAY: 3, Cedric Brown, Mike Washington & Jeris White; WASHINGTON: 9, Lemar Parrish.

TEAM CHAMPION
AFC: 34   Houston
NFC: 29   Chicago

TOP TEN INTERCEPTORS

	No	Yards	Avg.	Long	TD
Reinfeldt, Mike, Hou.	12	205	17.1	39	0
Parrish, Lemar, Wash.	9	65	7.2	23	0
Barbaro, Gary, K.C.	7	142	20.3	t70	1
Myers, Tom, N.O.	7	127	18.1	t52	1
Hayes, Lester, Oak.	7	100	14.3	t52	2
11 tied with	6				

AFC—INDIVIDUALS

	No	Yards	Avg	Long	TD
Reinfeldt, Mike, Hou.	12	205	17.1	39	0
Barbaro, Gary, K.C.	7	142	20.3	t70	1
Hayes, Lester, Oak.	7	100	14.3	t52	2
Wilson, J.C., Hou.	6	135	22.5	66	1
Nixon, Jeff, Buff.	6	81	13.5	43	0
Jauron, Dick, Cin.	6	41	6.8	12	0
Owens, Burgess, N.Y.J.	6	41	6.8	15	0
Lambert, Jack, Pitt.	6	29	4.8	23	0
Foley, Steve, Den.	6	14	2.3	7	0
Lowe, Woodrow, S.D.	5	150	30.0	t77	2
Green, Gary, K.C.	5	148	29.6	57	0
Darden, Thom, Clev.	5	125	25.0	t39	1
Preston, Ray, S.D.	5	121	24.2	35	0
Clark, Mario, Buff.	5	95	19.0	36	0
Colzie, Neal, Mia.	5	86	17.2	56	0
Small, Gerald, Mia.	5	74	14.8	40	0
Clayborn, Raymond, N.E.	5	56	11.2	27	0
Brown, Dave, Sea.	5	46	9.2	23	0
Shell, Donnie, Pitt.	5	10	2.0	8	0

t = touchdown

NFC — INDIVIDUALS

	No	Yards	Avg	Long	TD
Parrish, Lemar, Wash.	9	65	7.2	23	0
Myers, Tom, N.O.	7	127	18.1	t52	1
Lawrence, Rolland, Atl.	6	120	20.0	38	0
Lavender, Joe, Wash.	6	77	12.8	27	0
Stone, Ken, St. L.	6	70	11.7	30	0
Schmidt, Terry, Chi.	6	44	7.3	t20	1
Fencik, Gary, Chi.	6	31	5.2	17	0
Allen, Carl, St. L.	5	126	25.2	78	0
Cromwell, Nolan, L.A.	5	109	21.8	34	0
Youngblood, Jim, L.A.	5	89	17.8	t34	2
Gray, Johnnie, G.B.	5	66	13.2	35	0
Hicks, Dwight, S.F.	5	57	11.4	29	0
Hannon, Tom, Minn.	4	85	21.3	52	0
Wilson, Brenard, Phil.	4	70	17.5	50	0
Hughes, Pat, N.O.	4	62	15.5	40	0
Felton, Eric, N.O.	4	53	13.3	53	0
Wright, Nate, Minn.	4	44	11.0	32	0
O'Steen, Dwayne, L.A.	4	42	10.5	36	0
Williams, Gerard, S.F.	4	38	9.5	22	0
Bradley, Luther, Det.	4	11	2.8	11	0
Allen, Jimmy, Det.	4	0	0.0	0	0

PUNTING

YARDS PER PUNT
AFC: 43.6 Bob Grupp, Kansas City (89 punts, 3883 yards)
NFC: 42.7 Dave Jennings, New York Giants (104 punts, 4445 yards)

NET AVERAGE
AFC: 37.2 Bob Grupp, Kansas City (90 total punts, 3348 net yards)

NFC: 36.7 Dave Jennings, New York Giants (104 total punts, 3818 net yards)

LONGEST
AFC: 74 yards Bob Grupp, Kansas City vs. San Diego, November 4

NFC: 74 yards Mike Bragg, Washington vs. New York Giants, November 25

PUNTS
NFC: 104 Dave Jennings, New York Giants
AFC: 99 Bucky Dilts, Baltimore

TEAM CHAMPION
AFC: 43.1 Kansas City
NFC: 42.7 New York Giants

TOP TEN PUNTERS

	Punts	Yards	Long	Avg
Grupp, Bob, K.C.	89	3883	74	43.6
Jennings, Dave, N.Y.G.	104	4445	72	42.7
Guy, Ray, Oak.	69	2939	71	42.6
White, Danny, Dall.	76	3168	73	41.7
McInally, Pat, Cin.	89	3678	61	41.3
Evans, Johnny, Clev.	69	2844	59	41.2
Partridge, Rick, N.O.	57	2330	61	40.9
Ramsey, Chuck, N.Y.J.	73	2979	64	40.8
Parsley, Cliff, Hou.	93	3777	59	40.6
Beverly, David, G.B.	69	2785	65	40.4

PUNT RETURNS

YARDS PER RETURN
NFC: 11.4 John Sciarra, Philadelphia (16 returns, 182 yards)
AFC: 10.9 Tony Nathan, Miami (28 returns, 306 yards)

AFC: 612   J.T. Smith, Kansas City
NFC: 431   Danny Reece, Tampa Bay

RETURNS

NFC: 70   Danny Reece, Tampa Bay
AFC: 58   J.T. Smith, Kansas City

LONGEST

AFC: 88 yards   J.T. Smith, Kansas City vs. Oakland,
    September 23 (TD)
NFC: 77 yards   Lee Nelson, St. Louis vs. Chicago, December 16;
    Steve Schubert, Chicago vs. Detroit, November 4 (TD)

TOUCHDOWNS

AFC: Nesby Glagow, Baltimore vs. New England, November 18 (75
    yards); Stanley Morgan, New England vs. Baltimore, November
    18 (80 yards); Tony Nathan, Miami vs. Buffalo, October 14 (86
    yards); J.T. Smith, Kansas City vs. Houston, September 16 (55
    yards); vs. Oakland, September 23 (88 yards)
NFC: Steve Schubert, Chicago vs. Detroit, November 4 (77 yards)

TEAM CHAMPION

AFC: 10.6   Kansas City (58 returns, 612 yards)
NFC: 9.5   Philadelphia (57 returns, 544 yards)

TOP TEN PUNT RETURNERS

	No	FC	Yards	Avg	Long	TD
Sciarra, John, Phil.	16	0	182	11.4	38	0
Nathan, Tony, Mia.	28	14	306	10.9	t86	1
Smith, J.T., K.C.	58	10	612	10.6	t88	2
Hall, Dino, Clev.	29	5	295	10.2	47	0
Upchurch, Rick, Den. . . .	30	4	304	10.1	44	0
Morgan, Stanley, N.E. . .	29	21	289	10.0	t80	1
Fuller, Mike, S.D.	46	7	448	9.7	27	0

	No	FC	Yards	Avg	Long	TD
Schubert, Steve, Chi. ...	25	10	238	9.5	t77	1
Henry, Wally, Phil.	35	7	320	9.1	34	0
Smith, Jim, Pitt.	16	1	146	9.1	38	0

Leaders based on average return, minimum 16 returns

AFC — INDIVIDUALS

	No	FC	Yards	Avg	Long	TD
Nathan, Tony, Mia.	28	14	306	10.9	t86	1
Smith, J.T., K.C.	58	10	612	10.6	t88	2
Hall, Dino, Clev.	29	5	295	10.2	47	0
Upchurch, Rick, Den. ...	30	4	304	10.1	44	0
Morgan, Stanley, N.E. ..	29	21	289	10.0	t80	1
Fuller, Mike, S.D.	46	7	448	9.7	27	0
Smith, Jim, Pitt.	16	1	146	9.1	38	0
Harper, Bruce, N.Y.J. ...	33	9	290	8.8	51	0
Bell, Theo, Pitt.	45	7	378	8.4	27	0
Moody, Keith, Buff.	38	10	318	8.4	32	0

NFC — INDIVIDUALS

	No	FC	Yards	Avg	Long	TD
Sciarra, John, Phil.	16	0	182	11.4	38	0
Schubert, Steve, Chi. ...	25	10	238	9.5	t77	1
Henry, Wally, Phil.	35	7	320	9.1	34	0
Arnold, John, Det.	19	4	164	8.6	27	0
Hardeman, Buddy, Wash.	24	7	207	8.6	52	0
Mauti, Rich, N.O.	27	13	218	8.1	33	0
Wilson, Steve, Dall.	35	12	236	6.7	-13	0
Harrell, Willard, St. L. ..	32	12	205	6.4	68	0
Solomon, Freddie, S.F. .	23	2	142	6.2	14	0
Reece, Danny, T.B.	70	1	431	6.2	17	0

t = Touchdown

KICKOFF RETURNS

YARDS PER RETURN
AFC: 25.9 Larry Brunson, Oakland (17 returns, 441 yards)
NFC: 25.1 Jimmy Edwards, Minnesota (44 returns, 1103 yards)

YARDS
AFC: 1158 Bruce Harper, New York Jets
NFC: 1103 Jimmy Edwards, Minnesota

RETURNS
AFC: 55 Bruce Harper, New York Jets
David Turner, Cincinnati
NFC: 44 Jimmy Edwards, Minnesota
Steve Odom, Green Bay - New York Giants

LONGEST
NFC: 106 yards Roy Green, St. Louis vs. Dallas, October 21 (TD)
AFC: 104 yards Ira Matthews, Oakland vs. San Diego, October 25 (TD)

TOUCHDOWNS
AFC: Ira Matthews, Oakland vs. San Diego, October 25 (104 yards)
NFC: Billy Campfield, Philadelphia vs. Detroit, December 2 (92 yards); Roy Green, St. Louis vs. Dallas, October 21 (106 yards); James Owens, San Francisco vs. Denver, November 18 (85 yards); Aundra Thompson, Green Bay vs. New York Jets, November 4 (100 yards); Rickey Watts, Chicago vs. St. Louis, December 16 (83 yards)

TEAM CHAMPION
AFC: 22.7 Oakland (65 returns, 1475 yards)
NFC: 22.7 St. Louis (71 returns, 1609 yards)

TOP TEN KICKOFF RETURNERS

	No	Yards	Avg	Long	TD
Brunson, Larry, Oak.	17	441	25.9	89	0

Edwards, Jimmy, Minn	44	1103	25.1	83	0
Matthews, Ira, Oak.	35	873	24.9	t104	1
Green, Roy, St. L.	41	1005	24.5	t106	1
Owens, James, S.F.	41	1002	24.4	t85	1
Henry, Wally, Phil.	28	668	23.9	53	0
Arnold, John, Det.	23	539	23.4	69	0
Owens, Artie, S.D.	35	791	22.6	40	0
Harrell, Willard, St. L.	22	497	22.6	53	0
Nathan, Tony, Mia.	45	1016	22.67	43	0

AFC — INDIVIDUALS

	No	Yards	Avg	Long	TD
Brunson, Larry, Oak.	17	441	25.9	89	0
Matthews, Ira, Oak.	35	873	24.9	t104	1
Owens, Artie, S.D.	35	791	22.6	40	0
Nathan, Tony, Mia.	45	1016	22.6	43	0
Glasgow, Nesby, Balt.	50	1126	22.5	58	0
Clark, Allan, N.E.	37	816	22.1	38	0
Anderson, Larry, Pitt.	34	732	21.5	44	0
Ellender, Richard, Hou.	24	514	21.4	35	0
Harper, Bruce, N.Y.J.	55	1158	21.1	52	0
Belton, Horace, K.C.	22	463	21.0	52	0

NFC — INDIVIDUALS

	No	Yards	Avg	Long	TD
Edwards, Jimmy, Minn.	44	1103	25.1	83	0
Green, Roy, St. L.	41	1005	24.5	t106	1
Owens, James, S.F.	41	1002	24.4	t85	1
Henry, Wally, Phil.	28	668	23.9	53	0
Arnold, John, Det.	23	539	23.4	69	0
Harrell, Willard, St. L.	22	497	22.6	53	0
Walterscheid, Len, Chi.	19	427	22.5	44	0
Mauti, Rich, N.O.	36	801	22.3	39	0
Hammond, Bobby, N.Y.G.-Wash.	25	544	21.8	39	0
Odom, Steve, G.B.-N.Y.G.	44	949	21.6	75	0